tuck 'n' twist

by

Annie Tuley

Annie Tuley began sewing when she was five years old, and the love affair with fabrics, needles and threads has never stopped. She lectures and teaches in the Pittsburgh, Pennsylvania area where she lives with her supportive husband, Rick, and two children, John 8 and Kate 3 1/2. Her award winning work has been exhibited internationally, and is in private and corporate collections.

Published by **Clotilde** Inc.

Published in Ft. Lauderdale, FL 33315
by Clotilde Inc.

ISBN 0-9636715-0-2
Library of Congress Catalog Card
Number

TUCK 'N' TWIST

Making tucks has always been something I have shied away from. The fabric had to be perfectly marked, folded and stitched for good results. No matter how hard I tried, my work was never satisfactory. It was interesting, had potential, but also lacked the kind of precision I like. Then to add insult to injury if I didn't like what I had done, I had to pick out all those stitches, which seemed to take somewhere between forever and eternity.

Then came the Perfect Pleaters®. Now I make tucks and pleats quickly and perfectly; no marking, sewing or mistakes. The uses seem endless, but far and away my favorite thing is tucking stripes. I love taking a stripe and seeing the new patterns emerging under my fingertips, magically transforming one piece of fabric into something completely different, adding movement and texture in the process. If I don't like what I see or want to try another idea, I can just

pull the undamaged fabric out of the Pleater and start over. If it looks interesting, I can set the tucks and quickly create new tucked yardage.

The fun doesn't stop here. The tucks can be further manipulated by twisting and smocking, adding illusions, more texture and some wonderful "Conceal and Reveal" effects. The possibilities are truly endless!

This roomy, comfortable jacket is the perfect place to flaunt your creativity. The pattern pieces are all large and simple, with very few construction details — perfect for bulky manipulated fabrics. While this jacket fits into the wearable art genre, it is very **wearable**. (Of course! I'm horribly practical, why make a jacket that you can't use?) While the instructions given are only for a Tuck 'N' Twist jacket, this pattern also works well with other heavy fabrics such as quilted cottons and fake furs.

FABRIC SELECTION

The most important element is the stripe. Without the right kind and size, nice even tucks won't make much difference. First one must consider color. Okay, we're all lousy with color, but there are some basic things here that will make your work more successful. Please, these are only guidelines, things that I have seen work well. However, don't hesitate to try some piece of fabric that just begs to go home with you.

When tucking stripes the most important aspect of color is contrast—light versus dark. Extremely high contrast, such as black and white, can create illusions that dance and gyrate before the eyes when the two are in equal quantities. However, mostly black with narrow white stripes, or the other way around works very well. This is also true of bright vibrant colors, for example, fuchsia, turquoise and some greens. But by having some spacing with white, black or gray, they are toned down and behave better. The fabric used in this jacket is a good example of this. The charcoal gives a place for the bright stripes to play, yet keeps them from overwhelming the designs that emerge when tucked. The eye can distinctly see the patterns that develop without undue dancing about.

Low contrast, gray and light gray for example, can be very subtle, almost too subtle. Bright colors lend an air of playfulness; they are more sporty and flamboyant. Muted colors are quieter and more casual, perfect for jeans, better perhaps for everyday wear.

The texture of the fabric also changes things. Cottons, which are easier to work with, have a matte finish. Synthetics have a variety of finishes, such as shiny, leather look, or jacquard. These fabrics can be tamed with spray starch, but you will probably want to wash this out before actually wearing the garment. The synthetics lend a look of elegance and are sometimes worth the difficulties in handling them.

The fabric itself must be washable, able to withstand some heavy duty pressing (no cool-iron-only fabric), and able to hold a crease. This rules out some synthetics. Cottons work beautifully—chambray, calico/broadcloth weight and lightweight denims. In general, shirt weights are good, they have enough body to hold pleats without having the pleats flop down. Obvious no-no's are flimsy chiffons and laces and heavy denim or fake fur on the other end of the scale. But please, please, prewash and preshrink your selection. Finally, if you don't like the colors or feel you don't look good in them, you will never wear your jacket. The jacket is too good to hide in a dark closet so keep looking until you find what you really like. The right fabric is out there waiting for you.

STRIPES

Now that you know what type of fabric to look for, let's discuss stripes. This is make-it or break-it time. Some work, some don't. Again, these are merely guidelines, not absolutes. Every stripe is different and the final decision is yours.

There are many kinds of patterns in stripes. The widths between stripes can vary; however, the distance from the center line of one dominant stripe to the next should be almost equal across the piece of fabric and be somewhere between one and three inches wide. I try to avoid the printed border stripes as they are usually too variable in their widths. Also, I have found that there doesn't seem to be enough contrast and change in colors to work well for this purpose. Study the examples given. The comments should help steer you in the direction you want.

There is really only one sure way to tell if and how a stripe is going to work — try it. When I go out, I take my Pleaters with me. I leave them in the car so they won't be soiled but if I see something really interesting, I can try it out before purchasing a lot of yardage. You may feel a bit embarrassed about hauling a Pleater around a store. I did until the yards of striped fabric that I can't use in the Pleaters built up in my stash. Also, you look like you **know** what you are doing when you start trying, finding and rejecting fabric at the store — even if you really don't.

This stripe is composed of two colors in equal amounts. It has limited uses. It is best in a Conceal and Reveal type of manipulation. Using this for Angled Stripes variation causes the illusion of gyration. It doesn't let the eye really settle down and look at the design. This effect is often not desirable.

This piece of fabric falls into the fat/ thin genre. The red and yellow stripes are dominant, but not over-whelming. The narrow blue stripes add subtle undercurrents as they almost blend in with the wide stripe. Nice, but not a knock-em-dead piece.

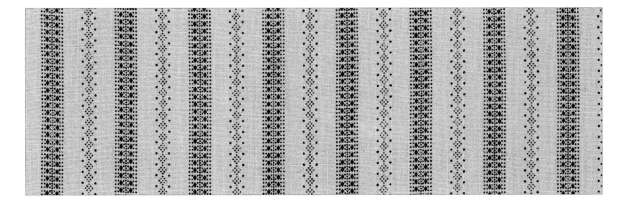

The distance between the stripes on this make it most suitable for the 22" Extra Long Pleater. It's super for small items such as purses and small children's clothes, but it's lost on larger items. I call this a fancy #1 /plain/ fancy #2 /plain. The pattern in the stripe breaks up the possible gyrations that occur when high contrasting colors are present in equal amounts. This is a good size to buy if you just want to experiment! It only takes a yard or so to get a wide variety of manipulation.

The softer, more romantic look can be achieved with this fat/thin stripe. The contrast here isn't as much in color as in design. It is very pleasant, without being daring. It is suited to crafts and accessories (such as handbags); okay for children's clothing instead of adult garments.

This flat/thin #1/ fat/thin #2 has all kinds of potential! There are many exciting possibilities with the Conceal and Reveal type of manipulation. The distance between repeats allows for deep tucks that twist up oh-so-nicely. (A real bargain—it was only a $1.00 yard.)

This fat fancy/plain/ thin fancy/plain stripe was a gift from a very special friend. The subtle colors give this piece an elegant richness. To enhance this I plan to add gold. The repeat is far enough apart for some nice deep tucks, yet still works very well for the Angled Stripe manipulations.

This stripe is just plain fun! It's bright, crazy, and screaming with potential. Tone it down, by using it in small areas—not in an entire garment. Kids love this one. (If you think this is bright I have it in neon too!)

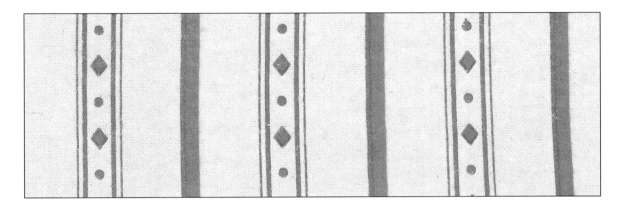

While this fat/thin/ fat/fancy stripe is flannelette, it still works very well. The neon colors might be too bright, but who really cares in the dark?

The contrast between the two stripes in this fabric is too subtle. When tucked and twisted it merely adds shadow and light to a relative solid. While this stripe has its use, don't spend much time experimenting with it for the Tuck 'N' Twist jacket.

Color separation between stripes is essential in this example; the separation between stripes is almost non-existent. The manipulations tend to disappear, leaving a very choppy indistinguishable look to any patterns created.

I love this border stripe. It works well in many places, but unfortunately not with this jacket; the widths of the stripes are too variable and the color contrast is insufficient.

Fortunately, this was on sale so I'm not out very much money. The width of the stripes changes too much within the repeat. I tried to use a different depth for each tuck depending on the stripe I was using but each stripe blended in too much with the next one. I still have plans for this fabric but not for the Tuck 'N' Twist jacket.

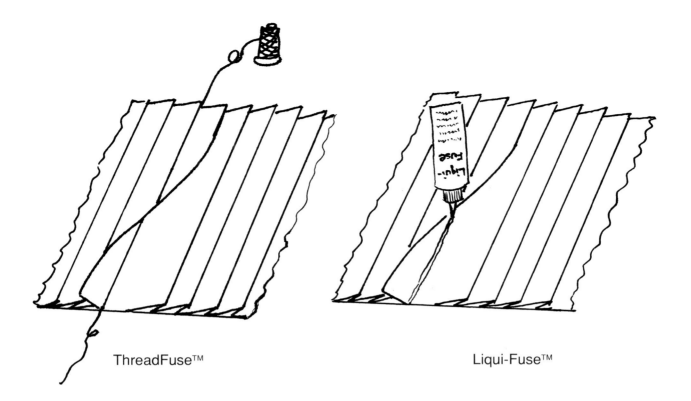

ThreadFuse™   Liqui-Fuse™

I put ThreadFuse or Liqui-Fuse inside the crease of each tuck when working with the narrower tucks. This helps maintain a nice crisp crease after washing. Vinegar doesn't set creases in natural fibers, so I use the fusible materials with cotton fabrics. Iron a fusible tricot interfacing onto the **wrong** side and peel off the freezer paper (you may use this paper again). Your newly manipulated stripe is now ready to go into your project.

When making tucked yardage you are not limited by the width of the Pleater. After ironing on the freezer paper, but before putting anything inside the tucks, realign the last tuck or two. Remember, when realigning the tucks, always start in the second louver and continue to pleat. Press on more freezer paper, remove from Peater and keep pleating as long as necessary. Then do the fusing steps all at once. If your tucked piece ends up too narrow, add more width by sewing on another piece of fabric, carefully matching the stripes. If possible, hide the seam inside the tuck.

Conceal and Reveal

For all the Conceal and Reveal types of manipulations, the stripe runs in the same direction as the louvers of the Pleater. First, a portion of the stripe is hidden inside the tuck, then exposed when the tuck is twisted back on itself and stitched down. I use Invisible Nylon Wonder Thread so the stitching doesn't show. The rows of stitching can be parallel to each other, at oblique angles to the tucks, or they can be in undulating rows.

Conceal and Reveal #1

For the left front of the jacket I used the 27" Skirt Pleater. The entire colored portion of each stripe was exposed, with the edge of it lined up with the edge of the louvers. The fabric looked about the same, only with a lot less gray between the colors.

After preparing the fabric for further manipulation (as outlined on the previous pages), I stitched all the tucks down straight across the top in the direction of the tucks, then turned the fabric around and stitched back straight across, except I twisted the tucks backwards, covering up the colored portion. I then turned and stitched the twisted tucks into their original position thus, in turn, showing and hiding different parts of the fabric.

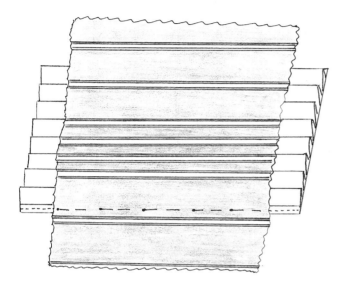

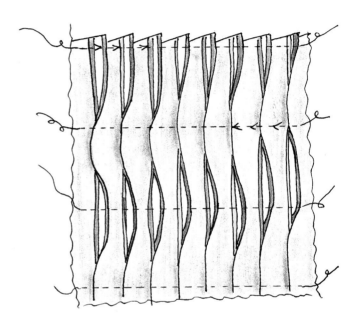

Conceal and Reveal #2

The 27" Skirt Pleater was used for the center back. I lined up the edge of the purple and yellow stripe so that it was along the edge of the first louver. The fabric was then tucked into the next louver until the purple and yellow stripe was barely covered leaving only the gray visible.

It was quite a pleasant surprise when the purple and yellow stripe peeked out. It really gives the piece more depth. The tucks were twisted in an undulating pattern, adding to the dynamics.

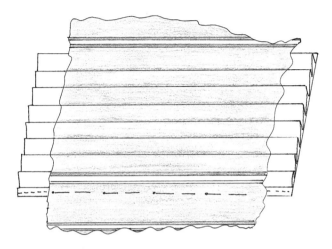

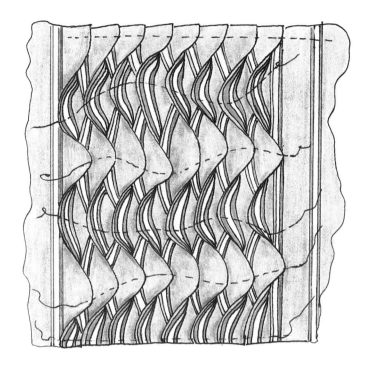

The pink and green stripe was on the opposite side of the gray, so I knew that this stripe would show quite clearly when the tuck was twisted.

Conceal and Reveal #3

The front of the left sleeve was made the same as Conceal and Reveal #2, except the purple and yellow stripe was lined up with the edge of the louver, then tucked in, barely concealed by the gray.

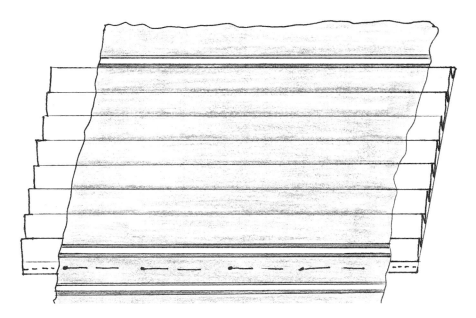

This forced the pink and green stripe deeper into the tuck, making it less visible after the tucks are twisted. Generally, the deeper the tuck, the more interesting the final outcome as you can hide and expose more. The depth and heights of the twisted tucks adds a great deal of visual impact also.

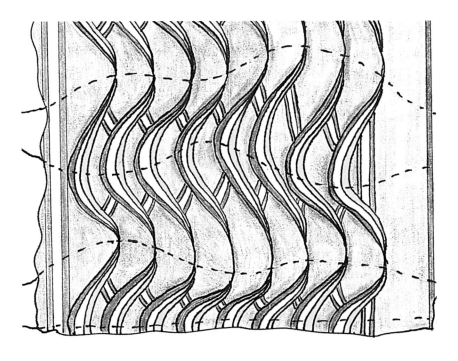

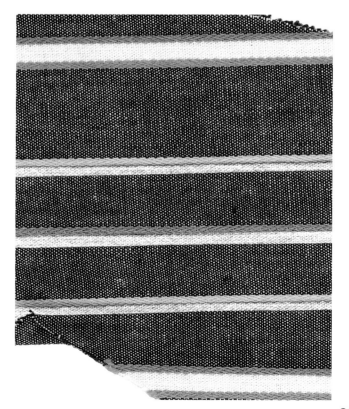

Honeycomb

For the upper back of the left sleeve, I used the 22" Extra Long Pleater tucking the gray stripe all the way into every third louver, with the edge of the louver barely covering the leading edge of the stripes.

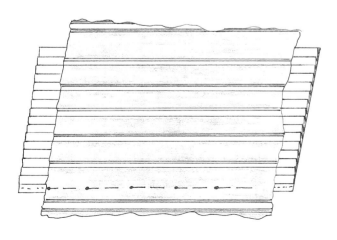

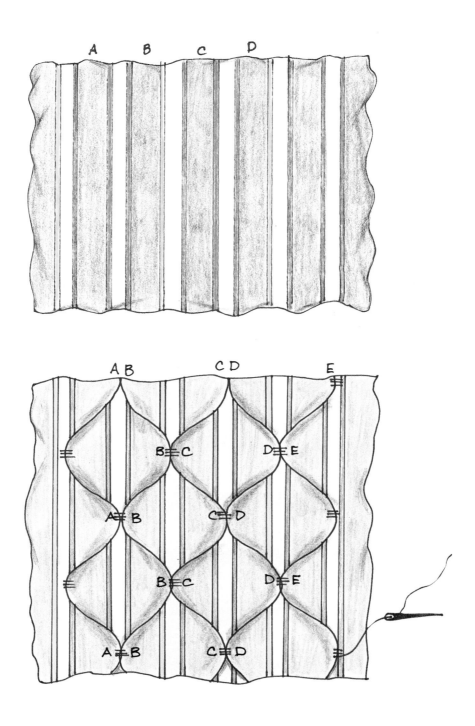

The tucks were pressed back and forth to make them stand up. I marked the edge of each tuck at one-inch intervals with a washout marker. Working from the top left, the first two tucks were whip-stitched together (A to B), then tied off. I continued across the row, stitching (C to D), and continued across the entire top. For the next row, two tucks, one from each of the above two pair were stitched together (B to C), for the width of the piece. And so on, for the entire piece.

VISUAL ILLUSION

An apparent visual illusion where the stripes appear to be converging on each other can be made by using the straight of the grain. Using either Pleater, depending on the desired depth, pleat the fabric with the stripes perpendicular to the louvers. Make sure that the stripes stay straight. This will look like your original stripe, only with little fold lines.

When twisting the tucks, I followed the white or center portion of each stripe. This gave an optical illusion of converging and diverging lines when viewed from the correct angle.

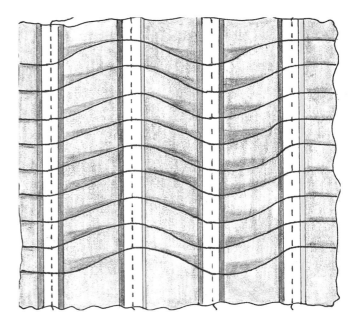

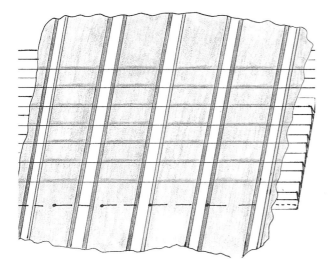

For the upper right front of the jacket, the stripe was lined up perpendicular to the louvers of the 22" Extra Long Pleater, pleated and tucked full depth into every other one. This looked just like the unpleated striped fabric, except with little fold lines running across the fabric.

ANGLED STRIPES

The last manipulations are made with the fabric at an angle. This creates wonderful directional changes. Try different angles to get different effects! Also try using different size pleats. Wonderful new patterns (much like Seminole piecing) can be made just by lining the stripes up in different ways. The tucks add an extra dimension that resewn strips do not have. I found that twisting these tucks broke up the new patterns too much with an already busy stripe. However, I have twisted them on other projects with other stripes and been quite satisfied with the results.

For all of the angled manipulations except the first one, I started with a corner of the fabric hanging down, and worked up. When the fabric became too wide for the Pleater, I just cut straight up, using the edge of the Pleater as a guide. This resulted in some odd shaped manipulated pieces and scraps.

These are just some ideas to get you started on tucked manipulation. There is always more than one way to do things. Get creative—you will come up with your own variations, some even quite different.

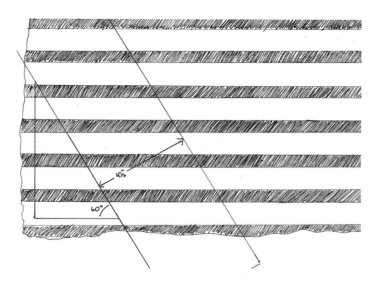

Angled Stripes #1

For the collar and the hipband, I used every other louver of the 22" Extra Long Pleater. The long strip of fabric was placed at right angles to the louvers and tucked so that the side of one stripe didn't quite touch the opposite side of the stripe from the previous tuck.

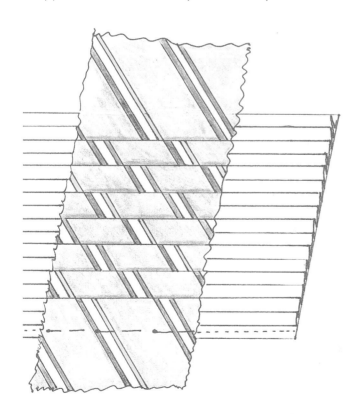

To get a piece of fabric long enough, I cut 4 1/2 inch strips at a 60° angle, pieced them, carefully matching the stripes, and pressed the seams open to reduce bulk. I just kept pleating until the piece fit the pattern.

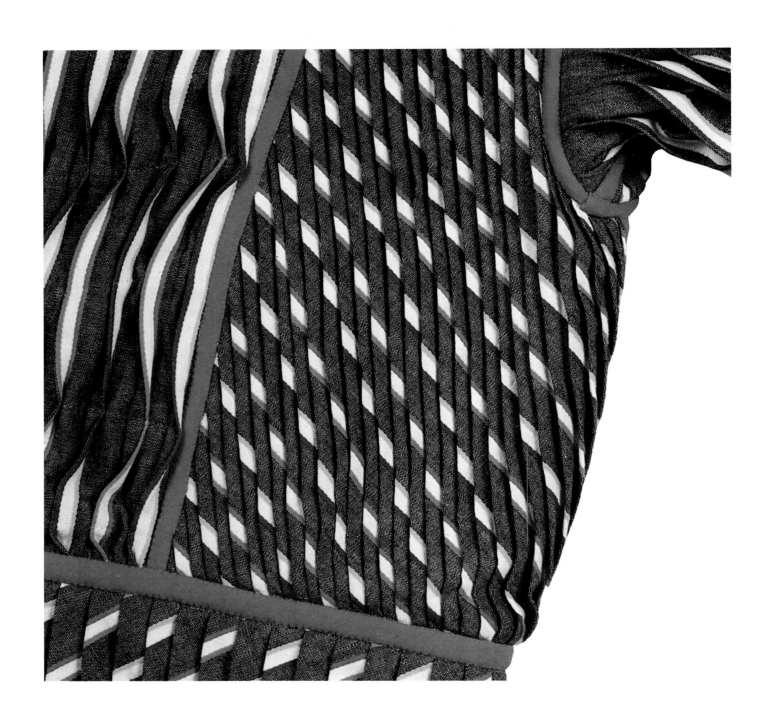

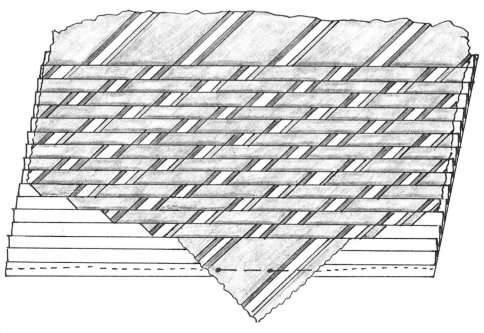

Angled Stripes #2

This piece goes around under the arm and to the back on the left side covering the underarm seam. It was also used on the lower right sleeve, only turned differently. I used every louver in the 22" Extra Long Pleater at a 45° angle with the stripe angled from the right. The stripes were tucked so that the outside of one stripe just touched the inside of the same stripe from the preceding tuck.

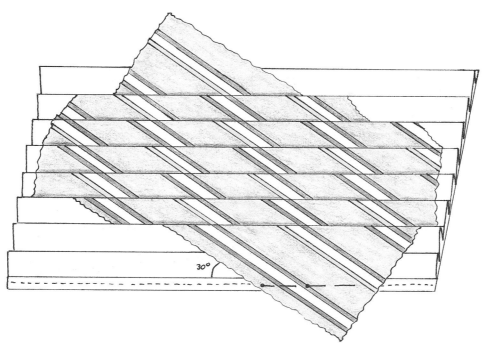

Angled Stripes #3

The left shoulder front and lower right front was made with the 27" Skirt Pleater, putting the stripe at a 30° angle to the louvers. For the first tuck, the pink portion of the green/white/pink stripe was lined up with the yellow portion of the yellow/white/purple stripe. This gives a jagged line, somewhat like an artist's drawing of lightning bolts.

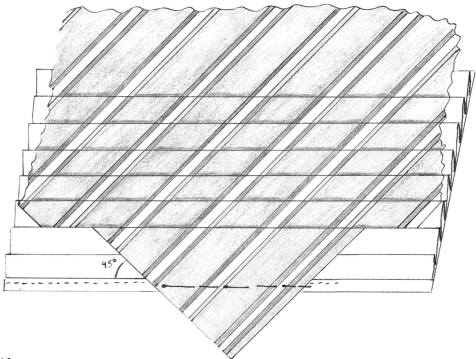

Angled Stripes #4

For the back of the lower left sleeve and the bottom right center front I used the 27" Skirt Pleater, using each louver. The fabric is pleated at a 45° angle. The stripe comes in from the right. Here I lined up the yellow/white/purple stripe with the pink/white/green stripe. It takes a second glance for the eye to realize that this isn't just a solid stripe, rather a stripe made up of two that are quite different.

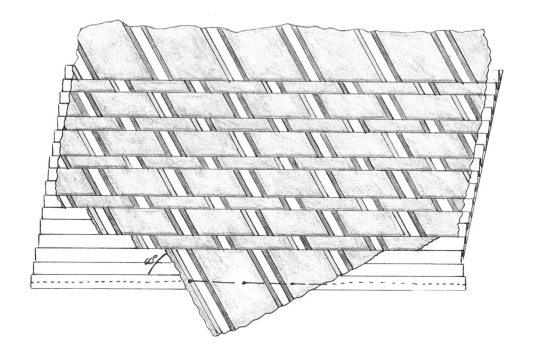

Angled Stripes #5

This last manipulation appears on the upper right sleeve. I used the 22" Extra Long Pleater, using two louvers and skipping the next for a narrow/wide effect. The stripe was brought in at a 60° angle from the left. The stripes themselves were centered between the previous row, creating an illusion of striped bits.

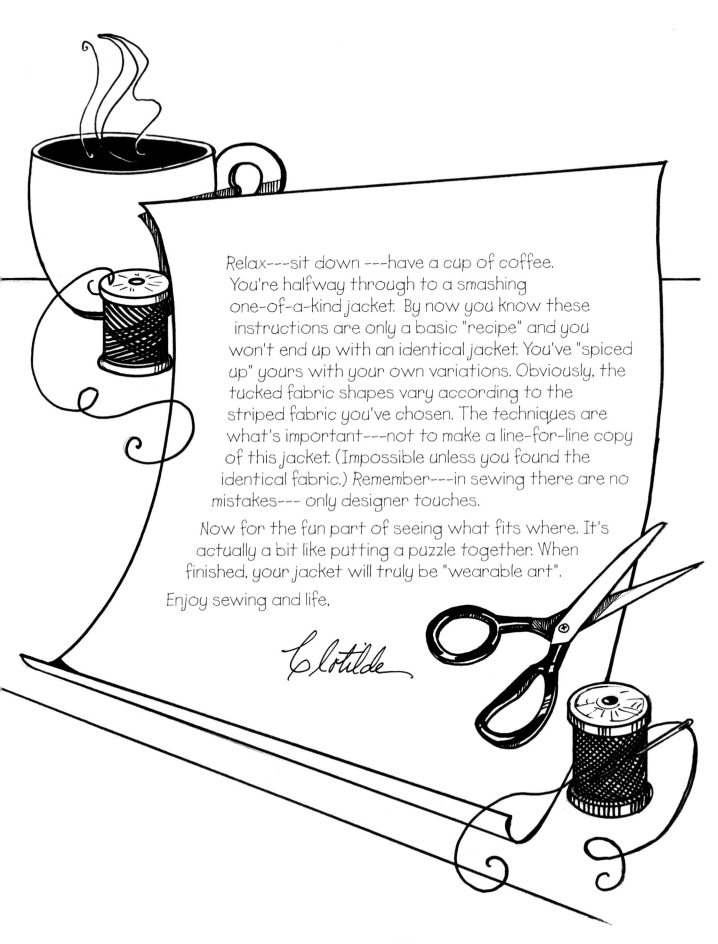

Relax---sit down ---have a cup of coffee. You're halfway through to a smashing one-of-a-kind jacket. By now you know these instructions are only a basic "recipe" and you won't end up with an identical jacket. You've "spiced up" yours with your own variations. Obviously, the tucked fabric shapes vary according to the striped fabric you've chosen. The techniques are what's important---not to make a line-for-line copy of this jacket. (Impossible unless you found the identical fabric.) Remember---in sewing there are no mistakes--- only designer touches.

Now for the fun part of seeing what fits where. It's actually a bit like putting a puzzle together. When finished, your jacket will truly be "wearable art".

Enjoy sewing and life,

Clotilde

PUTTING IT ALL TOGETHER

For the most part, I cut large pieces of random size and shape and manipulated them. The center back was originally intended for a sleeve so it was longer than the back of the pattern. So I just extended it over the shoulders into the front section. Some of the finished pieces had odd shapes due to the angling. Except for the hipband and collar, nothing was really planned and even those were afterthoughts based on what fabric I had left.

There wasn't enough fabric left to pleat the front facings or cuffs, so they are the original, unpleated stripe. (I even had to piece the facings!) We have added more yardage than I originally bought, just for this reason. You may decide not to tuck every piece anyway. If for some reason you come up short, work in a piece that contrasts or blends well, possibly from the bias strips. If you have fabric left over, you can make a matching handbag or yoke for a skirt to complete an outfit.

When determining where the various manipulations will go on the jacket, keep in mind how they will be viewed when the garment is actually worn. The direction of the apparent line in the tucked fabric is very important. Vertical lines tend to lengthen the body, horizontal lines tend to widen it. But also bear in mind that angles are very important too. If the visual lines tend to converge toward the waist, it can be very slimming—away from the waist and it can be most unflattering.

However, if the visual direction of the tucked fabric is less obvious, or the piece is small, it can be used to lead the eye to a more dramatic piece.

Balancing the different manipulations isn't as hard as it sounds. Look at what you have. While each piece has a life of its own, they all can, to a certain extent, be categorized. Some are Tuck 'N' Twist, others are Angled Stripes. The overall apparent direction sometimes is given by the visual impact of color, at other times by the direction of the lines of the tucks. This is another way of dividing up the pieces. But the important thing is to spread them all out, and mix to them—not all one kind on the left and the other on the right.

In general, the most dramatic piece tends to be the Conceal and Reveal with the deepest tucks. It is best when placed vertically so that the changes that occur when the piece is twisted and turned are viewed to the fullest advantage. This also puts the lines going up and down the body, adding visual length to both the jacket and its wearer.

If you have a big piece, put it on the back, as it is the largest unbroken area. Smaller pieces can go on the front, as it is broken up by the front opening or on the sleeves.

CONSTRUCTION INSTRUCTIONS

Pattern Layout and Cutting

Lay out the pattern pieces for the jacket underlining (flannelette) and lining according to the layout. The front facings, cuffs, one hipband and one collar should be cut out from the scraps of the striped fabric. If you have to piece anything, try to put the seams where they will be hidden, inside the cuff or on the lower portion of the facings.

When using batting, cut two full fronts, back and sleeves only. Note: Cut batting and lining 1" larger all the way around each pattern piece. This allows for shrinkage due to the quilting process.

Layout for lining. 44/45 fabric with or without nap. All Sizes.

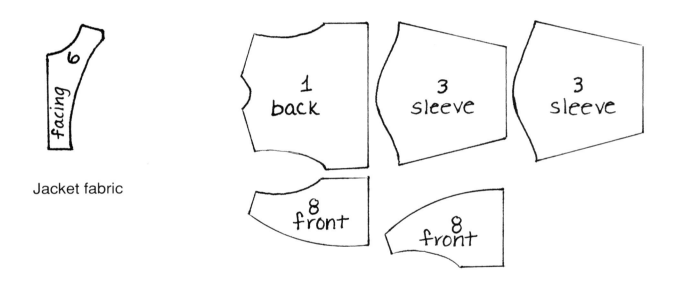

Jacket fabric

Layout for Flannelette Underlining. 44/45" fabric with or without nap. All Sizes.

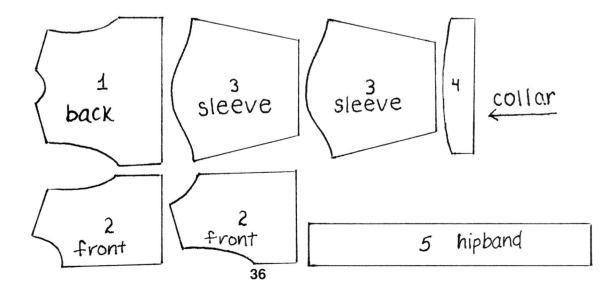

36

Layout of Tucked Sections

Sew the fronts and back of the flannelette together at the shoulders. Press the seams open. Lay the fronts, back and sleeves out on the floor or on a large table.

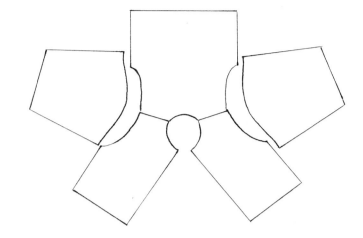

Start by putting the larger, more dramatic tucked pieces where they will be most visible, such as the back, center fronts, middle and top of the sleeves. Don't hide the best pieces under the arms! Let pieces extend over the shoulder seams. I also let the pieces from the front and back sides extend out far enough so that the side seams of the underlining will also be covered after this seam is sewn.

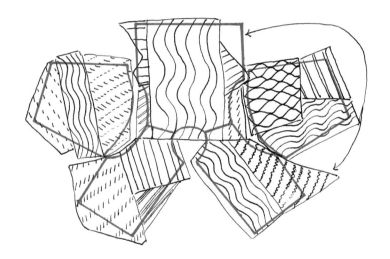

Once the major pieces are laid out, start filling in, crazy patch style, with the other tucked segments. Trim them as necessary. The pieces should overlap by at least 3/8 of an inch. The raw edges will be covered with bias strips so there is no need to turn them under. This eliminates much of the bulk when joining these pieces.

When you are satisfied with the placement of your tucked fabric, pin it all in place. (I put a rotary cutter mat or cardboard underneath the flannelette to prevent scratching the table or pinning everything to the carpet.) Stitch the side seams of the flannelette front and back, then cover these with the tucked fabric and pin in place. The front and back are now like a vest.

Zigzag over all the raw edges of the tucked fabric with a medium width (3.0) and length (1.5 or 14 stitches per inch). (A walking or even-feed foot eliminates shifting of several layers and is a real God-send, particularly with bulky and slippery fabrics.)

Stay stitch around the edges of the jacket. Work with the tucked fabric on the bottom. Zigzag just inside the raw edges of the flannelette.

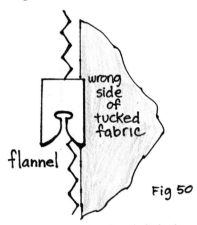

Fig 50

Trim away the excess tucked fabric, thus "cleaning up" around all the edges. If you are fortunate enough to have a serger, you can do this in one step.

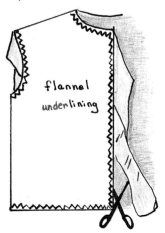

flannel underlining

For the sleeves, stay stitch 3/8 of an inch from the cut edge of the flannelette. Trim close to the stitching.

For the collar, place the tucked fabric right side **down**. Put the flannelette and then the untucked fabric right side **up** on top. Make sure that the markings on these two pieces match. Zigzag just inside the edges of the top layers. Trim away excess tucked fabric.

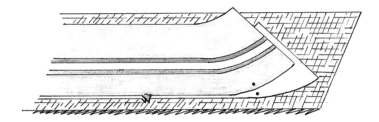

To prepare the hipband for construction, lay the flannelette piece on the wrong side of the tucked fabric. Stay stitch all around and cut off the excess tucked fabric. Match the hipband piece cut from the tucked strip to the flannelette-backed tucked piece. Stay stitch along the **bottom** edge only.

The cuffs use the "cheater" style of closing. I found that using tucked fabric made them too bulky. Gathering the sleeves to fit a cuff that fit over the wrist was also ruled out because there wasn't any other such fullness in the jacket for continuity. The "cheater" cuff keeps the sleeve sleek, which is more in keeping with the design of the rest of the jacket. Fusibly interface the cuff pieces. Stitch the side seams using a 5/8 inch seam allowance. Press the seams open. Fold the cuff in half right sides out, and stay stitch the raw edges together.

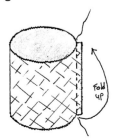

Fold up

Fold the cuffs in half with the seam on one side. Stitch a narrow tuck 1/8 inch from the fold line.

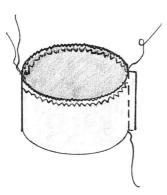

Turn both cuffs inside out. Stitch another narrow tuck, two inches from the inside one, taking care to make it two inches to the left on one cuff and two inches to the right on the other. These tucks make natural fold lines for the cuffs.

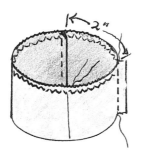

Bias Strips

Cut at least ten yards of strips 1 1/2 inches wide on the bias. Set aside 12" to make button loops. Cut 5 yards 2 1/4" wide; this is used to bind the jacket and sleeves. Fold the 1 1/2" strips in half **wrong** sides together and stitch 3/8 inches from folded edge.

The Fastube foot is great for stitching precise bias strips; just remember, use **right** sides out, **wrong** sides together. Trim all but a scant 1/8 inch of seam allowance off the edge of the tubes you just created. Insert a 3/8 inch wide Nylon Press Bar. Rotate the seam so that the stitching and seam allowances run down the center of the bar. Press.

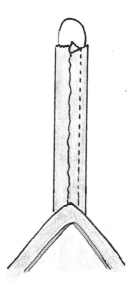

Move the bar down the tube as necessary, pressing as you go. Remove the bar, turn over and press. You now have strips of bias, ready to appliqué. The seam and seam allowances are underneath, where they will not show. (Note this is how to make bias strips for Celtic and stained glass quilt designs, as well as stems and vines in floral appliqué.)

To make the button loops, use 12 inches of the cut bias strips. Stitch **right** sides together, turn and press (using the Nylon Press Bar) with the seam in the center. If you have the Fasturn tubes, they make quick work of a tedious job. If not, use a safety pin. Pin it through the seam allowance. Put the pin into the tube and keep pushing it in, pulling the tube over it. Thread four to five strands of yarn into the turned tube to "stuff" it.

Appliquéing the Bias in Place

Appliqué the bias strips over the raw edges of the tucked fabric.

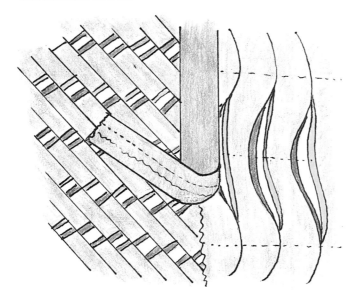

Stitch through all the layers of fabric. There are places where the edges of the strips will be covered by another strip, so do these first. If you choose to appliqué by hand, use a matching thread and whip or ladder-stitch. Be careful to catch all the layers. If you appliqué by machine, use Invisible Nylon Wonder Thread in the needle. It is a stretchy thread, so you will probably have to reduce your top tension.

There are a number of stitch options, the one you select will depend on your machine. When using a straight stitch, top stitch very close to the edge.

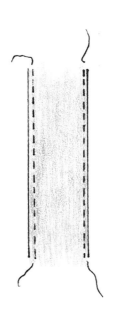

If you have a zigzag, use a 1.5 to 2.0 width and 1.5 to 2.0 (12 to 16 stitches per inch) length. Zig in the bias, zag off.

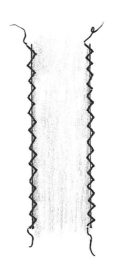

Many people use their blind hem stitch, or a pin stitch, reducing the width and length as necessary. With these two stitches, the straight part of the stitch is off the bias strip and the little bite just catches the piece being appliquéd.

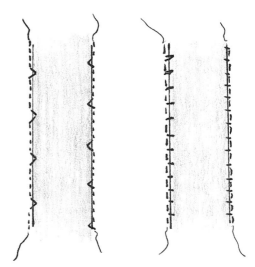

It may be easier to see what you are doing with an Open-Toe Embroidery or Satinedge Creative Foot. Good hand and machine appliqué should be barely visible and it should be hard to distinguish which is stitched by hand and which is by machine.

Assembling the Lining

I have found that spray-starching slippery fabric makes it much easier to work with. It not only tames the slinkiness, but stabilizes the bias and reduces fraying. The added body from the starch rinses away. Whether you starch or not depends on your fabric and your experience in dealing with them.

Stitch the front facings to the lining. If you have to piece the facings, try to do it closer to the bottom as this area does not show when the jacket is worn. Press seams toward the lining.

Stitch lining shoulder seams together, press seams open.

Using the flat construction method, stitch the sleeve lining to the armscye. Press toward the sleeve. Then stitch sleeve and side seams together using a 3/4 inch seam allowance. Press open.

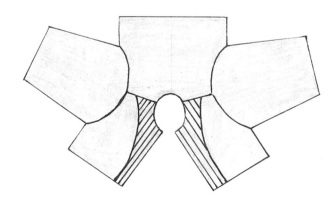

Gather the bottom of the jacket. Stitch on the hipband facing, matching all dots.

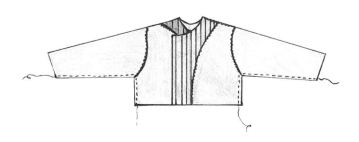

Putting It All Together

Overlap the underarm sleeve seam, right side out, and zigzag on top, next to the exposed raw edge. Sewing a regular seam creates too much bulk with all the tucks, so I avoid it when I'm making a garment with lots of fiber manipulations. Appliqué bias strips over the raw edges. (The bias strips not only cover the raw edges, but add a decorative element as well as separating the different elements.)

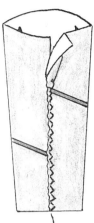

I find that it is much easier to put the cuffs on sleeves before the sleeves have been attached to the jacket or blouse and I do this whenever possible. This is no exception. Slip the cuff just inside the sleeve, with a 3/8 inch overlap. Match the cuff seam to the underarm seam. Stay-stitch, then cover the raw edges of the sleeve with the bias strips. The raw edge inside is going to be covered with the lining.

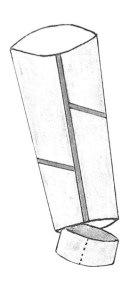

41

Mark 3/8 inch wide elastic according to dots on the hipband pattern. Match these up to the corresponding dots on the flannelette of the jacket. Stretch the elastic as you stitch it down (zigzag 3.0 width, 2.0 or 14 stitches per inch length).

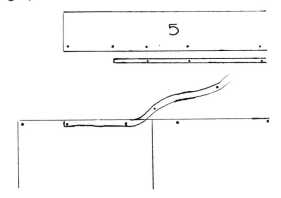

Set the sleeve into the armscye, matching the notches and dots. Zigzag over the raw edges; then apply the bias strips over them, starting and stopping at the underarm seam.

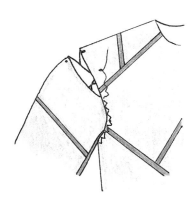

The bottom of the jacket has to be gathered a little bit to fit the hipband. I found that the easiest way to draw up all those layers in the tucks is to use elastic. The Invisible (or clear) Elastic works best as it doesn't "grow." It will return to its original length, even with the six layers of tucks, fusible web and flannelette. It doesn't care where you stitch in it or if it gets nicked. Nor does it seem to lose its stretch after repeated washings.

I found that it took a few minutes for the elastic to regain its original shape in this particular application. But it is certainly a lot easier than trying to adjust the gathers in all those layers. I also found that all the gathering tended to disappear in the tucks and is not really visible from the outside, giving the jacket an imperceptible fullness.

Place the lining inside the jacket taking care not to twist the sleeves. Baste in place around all raw edges except the sleeves. By hand, tack the lining to the jacket where the sleeve and side seams meet to prevent the lining from "wandering" during normal wear.

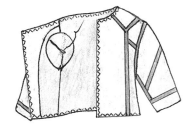

Fold under the raw edge of the sleeve lining and slip stitch to the cuff.

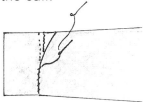

Using a 5/8 inch seam allowance and matching up all marks, sew the right side of the hipband facing to the bottom edge of the jacket, stitching through all layers. (The right side of the facing is on the right side of the lining.) Press the seam toward the facing.

Pin the tucked hipband to hipband facing **WRONG** sides together. Baste in place. Appliqué a long bias strip over this raw edge, stitching through all layers including the lining and hipband facing.

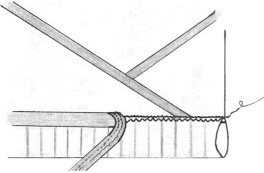

Trim off 1/4 inch to 3/8 inch of jacket neckline. Additional "fudging" may be necessary. (Remember, trimming enlarges the neckline.) Line up collar at center back and front edges. Overlap collar 1/4 inch alone neckline seam. Zigzag in place. Cover the raw edges of the neckline with appliquéd bias trim on the **outside** of the jacket.

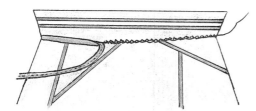

Then, with Invisible Nylon Wonder Thread in both the top and bobbin of the machine, appliqué the bias trim over the raw neckline edges on the **inside** of the jacket, using the previous stitching as a guideline for the bias. The collar turns down, and part of the facing is exposed. Since this portion is visible when worn, it is better to do it last.

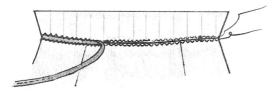

Applying the Binding

Whenever I am binding quilts or garments, I prefer to use a French binding. I have found that the double layer of fabric wears better, as well as smoothing the entire edge. This is particularly essential here with all the lumps and bumps created by the tucks. This binding is not only neater than the traditional binding, but it is also easier to apply.

There are two ways to put on the bias binding; "front-to-back" or "back-to-front" (this is normally used on quilts, hence the "back" and "front" terminology). Since I use the sewing machine as much as possible, I prefer the second method. However, try both out and select the one that you are most comfortable with. Bind all raw edges - the bottom of the hipband, up the fronts and around the collar. Also, for continuity, bind the folded edge of the cuffs.

For both methods, piece the 2 1/4 inch wide strips to create continuous binding.

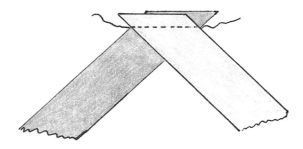

(The fastest way to create continuous binding is to cut all the bias strips the desired width with the rotary cutter, then piece them. It is also easier on the hands than the traditional method which requires a great deal of cutting with scissors.)

Fold the strip in half length-wise wrong sides together, matching the raw edges.

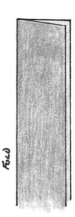

Method 1: Front to Back

Working on the outside of the jacket, line the edges of the continuous bias strip up with the raw edge being bound. Stitch 3/8 inch from the edge, mitering the corners as you go.

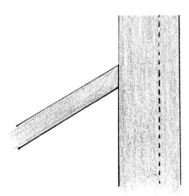

Wrap the bias over the edge of the jacket. Stitch the folded edge of the the bias down by hand, covering the line of machine stitching.

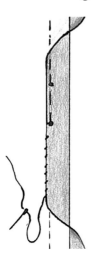

Method 2: Back to Front

Working on the **inside** of the jacket, apply the binding as in Method 1, wrapping the bias over to the outside of the jacket.

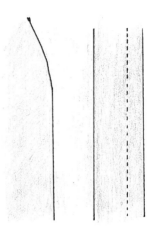

Machine appliqué the folded edge of the bias, just covering the previous stitching line.

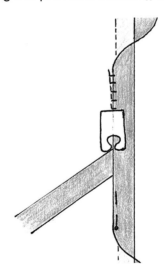

Button Loops

Stitch bias tube strip right sides together. Turn right side out. Securely stitch the button loops onto the centerfold of the cuffs and onto the edge of the hipband. Make sure that they are long enough to loop around the buttons.

Buttons

I could not find buttons in the right color so I made covered buttons. They are really quite easy. Just follow the directions on the package. The buttons on the cuffs were not very large or visible, so I used flat scraps from the bias binding. The button on the hipband was much larger so I made 1/4 inch stitched tucks. (The Pleater shouldn't be used to make these tucks as the interfacing would add too much bulk.) Using a disappearing or water-soluble marker, mark a piece of fabric with lines 3/4 inch apart.

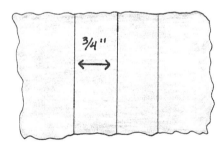

Fold along these lines and stitch 1/4 inch from the fold.

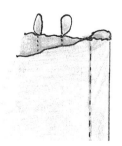

Press the tucks to one side. Then twist halfway down and press to the other side. Use this piece to make the button following the manufacturer's directions.

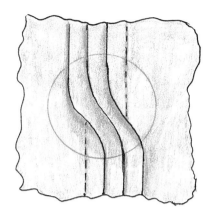

Put the jacket on to mark the button and jumbo snap locations on the hipband. Stitch in place. I put two jumbo snaps on the inside of the hipband, but buttons could have been used instead. This will maintain the overlap look and keep the band from shifting while wearing. These can also be repositioned over the years if needed... And now you are finished!

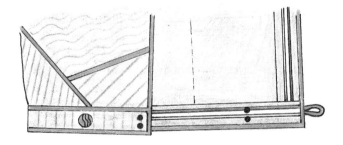

WEAR WITH PLEASURE!!!

Yardage:

Striped fabric *				
	45" wide	6 3/8 yds	6 3/4 yds	7 yds
	60" wide	4 3/4 yds	5 yds	5 1/4 yds
Flannelette	45" wide	2 7/8 yds	2 7/8 yds	3 yds
	30" wide	4 1/2 yds	4 1/2 yds	4 1/2 yds
Lining	45" wide	2 1/8 yds	2 1/4 yds	2 3/8 yds

Fusible Tricot Interfacing				
	60" wide	2 yds	2 yds	2 yds
	22" wide	6 yds	6 yds	6 yds

Thermore® Batting (optional) 1 queen size (90" x108") package

* Check the bargain tables first. The stripes that work best for this jacket are normally considered difficult to work with, so they don't sell well. Most of my best stripes (including this one) came from underneath piles of junk.

Notions:

Necessary:

Uncovered buttons

    2 -1 1/8 " uncovered buttons
    1 -1 1/2"uncovered button
    Invisible Nylon Wonder Thread
    3 yds Invisible Elastic
    2 Jumbo 1/2" snaps
    22" Clotilde's Extra Long Perfect Pleater®
    27" Clotilde's Skirt Perfect Pleater®

Very Helpful:

    Walking or Even Feed Foot
    Fasturn
    Fastube
    Nylon Bias Press Bars
    Rotary Cutter and Mat
    24" C-Thru Ruler®
    Satinedge Creative Foot™

Source for notions, Pleaters and Flannelette

If these notions, interfacing and flannelette are not available from your local fabric store, you can order them from Clotilde call 1-800-772-2891 for her **free** notions catalog.

Clotilde, Inc.
1909 S.W. First Ave.
Fort Lauderdale, FL 33315 -2100
1-800-772-2891

*Source for striped fabrics

The Quilt Shoppe
106 Wagner Drive
Bethel Park, PA 15102
412-835-6785

*The Quilt Shoppe carries a wide variety of striped fabrics selected specifically for the **Tuck 'N' Twist** projects. Call or write for swatches.

ISBN 0-9636715-0-2